Wicked Jokes for Wise Kids

With cartoons by
Lucy Jordan

Michael O'Mara Books Ltd

First published in Great Britain in 1999 by
Michael O'Mara Books Limited
9 Lion Yard, Tremadoc Road
London SW4 7NQ
This edition includes material from
The Mega Joke Book for Kids © 1997

ISBN 1-85479-459-0

Cover illustration by Phil Garner, Beehive Illustration

1 3 5 7 9 10 8 6 4 2

Printed and bound by Cox & Wyman, Reading

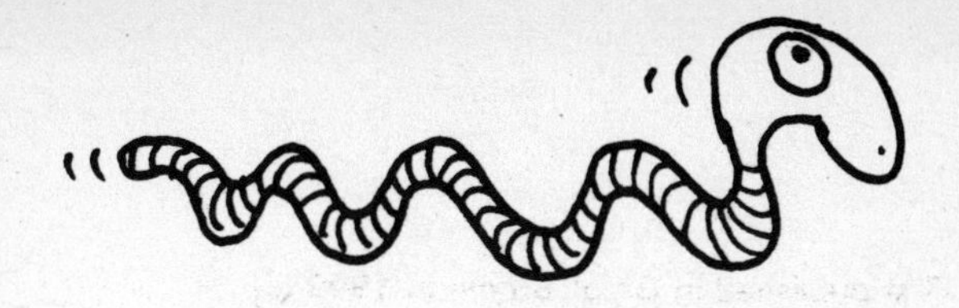

Contents

Animal antics

What do you get if you pour boiling water down a rabbit hole?
Hot cross bunnies.

What travels at 60 m.p.h. under water?
A motor pike and side carp.

It's raining cats and dogs.
I know. I just stepped in a poodle.

How do you stop your dog from digging in the garden?
Take away his spade.

Customer: Have you got a cod's head for the cat?
Fishmonger: Why, are you doing a transplant?

A man went into the pub and ordered a pint of lager for himself and one for his pet giraffe. The giraffe collapsed after its drink and another man came into the pub and said, 'What's that lyin' on the floor there, mate?' The man replied, 'Are you stupid? That's not a lion, it's a giraffe.'

What do you give a sick pig?
Oinkment.

What do you call a travelling flea?
An itch-hiker.

What do glow-worms eat?
Light snacks.

Mother kangaroo: I hate it when it rains and the kids have to play inside!

How many sheep does it take to make a sweater?
I didn't even know they could knit!

Woman: Can I have a parrot for my little girl.
Pet shop owner: I'm afraid I don't need any more little girls.

What do you get if you cross a parrot with a centipede?

A walkie-talkie.

One goldfish swimming in a goldfish bowl said to the other goldfish: 'Why do you keep following me around?'

Why did the bald man paint rabbits on his head?

Because from a distance they looked like hares.

What do you get if you cross a chicken with a cement-mixer?

A bricklayer.

What do you call a penguin in the desert?

Lost.

Does your dog bite?

No.

Ow! I thought you said your dog didn't bite!

He doesn't. That isn't my dog!

How do you stop your dog from barking in the hall.

Put him in the garden.

What animal always goes to bed with its shoes on?

A horse.

How do you stop a skunk from smelling?

Hold its nose.

What is a bear's favourite drink?

Coca-Koala.

What is black and white and noisy and smelly?

A skunk with a drumkit.

What's white and furry and smells of peppermint?

A Polo Bear.

What do you call a reindeer with one eye?

No idea.

What do you call a reindeer with one eye and no legs?

Still no idea.

A man was amazed to see a dog buying meat for his owner in a butcher's because not only did he appear to check the quality of the meat, but he noticed that the butcher short-changed him and growled until he was given the right money.

Intrigued, the man followed the dog from the shop and saw him help an old lady across the road with her shopping. The man then followed the dog to his owner's house and couldn't believe his eyes when the dog stood up on his hind legs to ring the doorbell.

The dog's owner came to the door, took the shopping from the dog and kicked him out into the garden. The man watching was horrified and called out to the owner,

'I can't believe you kicked that amazing dog – he does your shopping, checks your change and even helps old ladies across the road!' 'I know,' the owner replied, 'but that's the third time this week he's forgotten his keys.'

What did one flea say to the other as they came out of the nightclub?
'Shall we walk home or take a dog?'

Why shouldn't you play cards in the jungle?
Because there are too many cheetahs.

What is brown, prickly and squirts jam?
A hedgehog eating a doughnut.

Who tells the best chicken jokes?
Comedi-hens.

What happened to the cat who ate a ball of wool?
She had mittens.

When is the best time to buy budgies?
When they're going cheap.

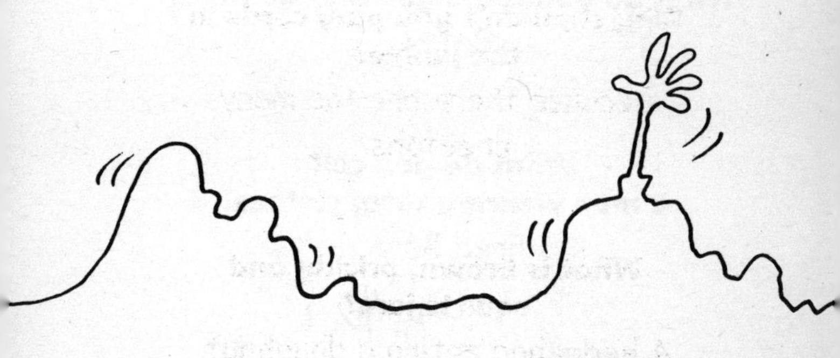

Crazy names

What do you call a woman with one leg shorter than the other?
Eileen.

What do you call a man driving a truck?

Laurie.

What do you call a girl who gambles?

Betty.

What do you call a man wearing tatty clothes?

Fred Bare.

What do you call a girl with one foot on either side of the river?

Bridget.

What do you call a man with a spade on his head?

Doug.

What do you call a girl with only one trouser leg?

Jean.

What do you call a man who's a talented painter?

Art.

What do you call a man with no arms and legs floating out to sea?

Bob.

What do you call a camel with no humps?

A horse.

What's green and holds up stagecoaches?

Dick Gherkin.

What do you call a camel with three humps?

Humphrey.

What do you call a man with a car on his head?

Jack.

What do you call a lady in the distance?

Dot.

Which famous explorer invented the peppermint?

Marc O'Polo.

Which famous mystery writer was smoky bacon flavoured?

Agatha Crispy.

What do you call a girl standing between two goal posts?

Annette.

What do you call a man in a pile of leaves?

Russell.

Who was Russia's most famous gardener?

Ivan Hoe.

What do you call a man with a seagull on his head?

Cliff.

What do you call a man who's always around when you need him?

Andy.

What do you call a boy who gets up your nose?

Vic.

What do you call a man with a wooden head?

Edward.

What do you call a man with a rabbit on his head?

Warren.

What do you call an Irishman with two panes of glass on his head?

Paddy O'Doors.

What do you call a man with a flashing blue light on his head?

Nick.

What do you call a girl with a frog on her head?

Lily.

What do you call a man in a plastic coat?

Mac.

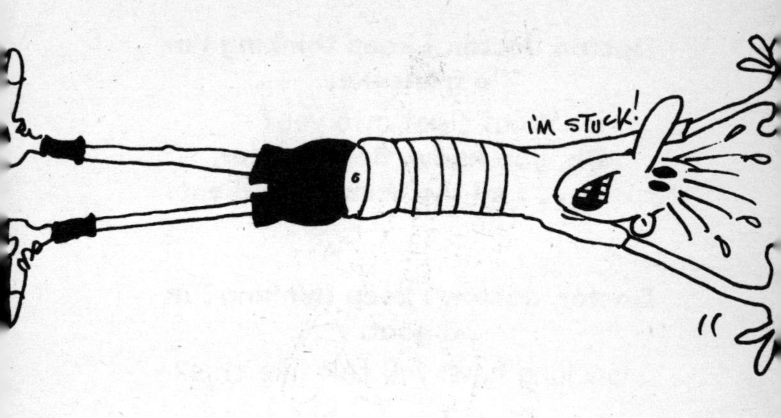

Doctor, doctor . . .

Doctor, doctor, I keep thinking I'm getting smaller.

Well, you'll just have to be a little patient.

Doctor, doctor, I keep thinking I'm a fruitcake.

What's got into you?

Oh, you know, flour, butter, raisins . . . all the usual ingredients.

Doctor, doctor, I keep thinking I'm a goat.

How long have you felt like this?

Since I was a kid.

Doctor, doctor, I've got jelly in one ear and custard in the other.

Don't worry, you're just a trifle deaf.

Doctor, doctor, I think I'm invisible.

Who said that?

Doctor, doctor, my hair keeps falling out. Can you give me something to keep it in?

How about this plastic bag?

Doctor, doctor, I can't help stealing things.

Please take a seat.

Doctor, doctor, my hands won't stop shaking.

Tell me, do you drink a lot?

No, I spill most of it.

Doctor, doctor, can you give me first aid?

No, I'm afraid you'll have to wait your turn.

Doctor, doctor, I feel like a pack of cards.

Take a seat and I'll deal with you later.

Doctor, doctor, I've been beaten up.

Have you got any scars?

No, I don't smoke.

Doctor, doctor, I keep getting this stabbing pain in my eye when I drink a cup of tea.

Try taking the spoon out.

Doctor, doctor, I keep forgetting things.

When did this start happening?

When did what start happening?

Doctor, doctor, I think I'm a spoon.

Stay quiet, get lots of rest and don't stir yourself.

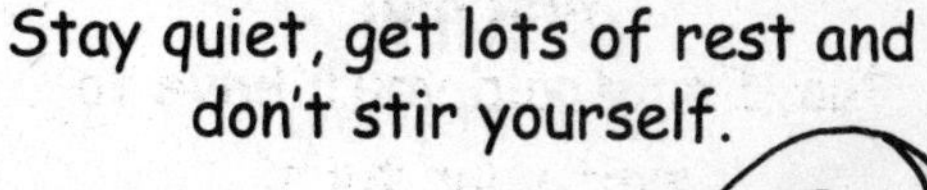

Doctor, doctor, I keep seeing big pink monsters with purple spots.

Have you seen a psychiatrist?

No, just big pink monsters with purple spots.

Doctor, doctor, what's the best cure for flat feet.

A foot pump.

Doctor, doctor, I feel like an apple.

Don't worry, I don't bite.

Doctor, doctor, I think I'm a dustbin.

Don't talk such rubbish.

School side-splitters

Teacher: Name a legendary creature that was half man and half beast.

Pupil: Buffalo Bill.

Teacher: When was the Iron Age?

Pupil: Before they invented drip-dry shirts?

Teacher: What can you tell me about the Dead Sea?

Pupil: I didn't even know it was ill.

Teacher: Why did cavemen paint pictures on cave walls?

Pupil: Because they couldn't spell their names.

Teacher: You should have been here at 9 o'clock!

Pupil: Why, what happened?

Teacher: This homework is in your father's writing.

Pupil: I know, sir, I borrowed his pen.

What do music teachers give you?

Sound advice.

Teacher: Can you tell me where elephants are found?

Pupil: How could anyone lose an elephant?

Teacher: What was the Romans' most remarkable achievement?

Pupil: Learning Latin.

Teacher: If you had £5 in one pocket and £2.45 in the other, what would you have?

Pupil: Someone else's trousers on, miss.

What word is always spelt incorrectly?

Incorrectly.

Teacher: Can you name two days of the week beginning with the letter 'T'?

Pupil: Today and tomorrow!

Teacher: The ruler of old Russia was called the Czar and his wife was called the Czarina. What were his children called?

Pupil: *Czardines?*

What did the chicken study in college?

Eggonomics.

Why did the thermometer go to college?

Because he wanted to get a degree.

Teacher: In the list of English monarchs, who came after Mary?

Pupil: Her little lamb?

Pupil: Please miss, would you punish someone for something they didn't do?

Teacher: No, of course not.

Pupil: Oh good, because I haven't done my homework.

Teacher: If you had 50p in one pocket and you asked your Dad for another 50p, what would you have?

Pupil: 50p.

Teacher: You obviously don't know how to add up.

Pupil: You obviously don't know my Dad!

Teacher: What comes after 'O' in the alphabet?

Class: 'K!'

Parent: I'm worried about you being at the bottom of the class.

Child: Don't worry, mum, they teach the same things at both ends.

Teacher: I wish you'd pay a little attention!

Pupil: I'm paying as little as I can, sir.

Pupil: Sir, why do teachers get paid when we have to do all the work?

Knock, knock jokes

Knock, knock.

Who's there?

Albert.

Albert who?

Albert you'll never guess.

Knock, knock.
Who's there?
Tank.
Tank who?
My pleasure!

Knock, knock.
Who's there?
Barbie.
Barbie who?
Barbie Q ready yet, I'm starving?

Knock, knock.

Who's there?

Alex.

Alex who?

Alex plain later, just let me in.

Knock, knock.

Who's there?

Luke.

Luke who.

Luke through the keyhole and you'll see.

Knock, knock.

Who's there?

Stan.

Stan who?

Stan back, I'm going to break the door down.

Knock, knock.

Who's there?

You.

You who?

Did you call?

Knock, knock.

Who's there?

Snow.

Snow who?

Snow good asking me, I can't remember.

Knock, knock.

Who's there?

Felix.

Felix who?

Felixtremely cold, can you let me in?

Knock, knock.

Who's there?

Watson.

Watson who?

Watson TV tonight?

Knock, knock.

Who's there?

Dozen.

Dozen who?

Dozen anyone know my name?

Knock, knock.

Who's there?

Hatch.

Hatch who?

Bless you.

Knock, knock.

Who's there?

Doctor.

Doctor who?

Yes, that's right. Tell me, have you seen my Tardis?

Knock, knock.

Who's there?

Liz.

Liz who?

Lizen carefully, I'm only going to say this once.

Knock, knock.

Who's there?

Cook.

Cook who?

That's the first one I've heard this year.

Knock, knock.

Who's there?

Hugo.

Hugo who?

Hugo and answer the telephone, I'll let myself in.

Knock, knock.

Who's there?

Althea.

Althea who.

Althea later, alligator.

Knock, knock.

Who's there?

Canoe.

Canoe who?

Canoe hurry up and let me in?

Knock, knock.

Who's there?

Avenue.

Avenue who?

Avenue learnt my name yet?

Knock, knock.

Who's there?

Dismay.

Dismay who?

Dismay be the wrong door, but can you let me in anyway.

Ghostly gags

What is Dracula's favourite landmark?
The Vampire State Building.

What do you call a wizard from outer space?
A flying sorcerer.

How does a vampire cross the ocean?
In a blood vessel.

What is a monster's favourite game?
Swallow my leader.

What do polite vampires always remember to say?
Fangs very much.

Why did the skeleton go to the party.
Because he wanted a rattling good time.

Did you hear about the cannibal with indigestion?
He ate someone who disagreed with him.

Why did Frankenstein have indigestion?
He bolted his food.

What is a ghost's favourite music?
A haunting melody.

What do cannibals eat at home?
Baked beings on toast.

What do polite monsters say at meal times?
Pleased to eat you.

What do cannibals eat at parties?

Buttered host.

What medicine do ghosts take for colds?

Coffin drops.

What do ghosts eat for dinner?

Ghoulash.

Why do vampires play poker?
Because the stakes are high.

What do short-sighted ghosts wear?
Spooktacles.

What do vampires put in their fruit salad?
Necktarines and blood oranges.

How did the two vampires fall in love?
Love at first bite.

What do you get if you cross Dracula with a hotdog?
A fangfurter.

Why does Dracula drink blood?
Because Diet Coke makes him burp.

What do ghosts put in their coffee?
Evaporated milk.

What do ghosts like on their roast beef?

Gravey.

What does a monster eat when he's just been to the dentist?

The dentist.

What does a postman deliver to ghosts?

Fang mail.

Chortle, chortle

What did the astronaut see in his frying pan?
An unidentified frying object.

Why did the biscuit cry?
Because his mother had been a wafer so long.

Why is a forest always full.
Because trees a crowd.

Why did the dinosaur cross the road?
Because chickens hadn't evolved yet.

There was an old woman from Leeds,
Who swallowed a packet of seeds.
In less than an hour,
Her nose grew a flower,
And her hair was all covered
in weeds.

Why did the man jump from the Empire State Building?

Because he wanted to make a hit on Broadway.

Why did the boy throw his clock out of the window?

To see time fly.

What do traffic wardens have in their sandwiches?

Traffic jam.

Why did the banana go out with the prune?

Because he couldn't find a date.

Did you hear about the stupid shoplifter?

He was found dead under Sainsbury's.

Who was the first underwater spy with a licence to kill?

James Pond.

If crocodile skins make a good pair of shoes, what do banana skins make?

Good slippers.

Who invented the first plane that couldn't fly?

The Wrong brothers.

What lives under the sea and carries a lot of people?

An octobus.

Which sixties pop group kills all known germs?

The Bleach Boys.

There was a young man
from Dungall,
Who went to a fancy dress ball.
He thought he would risk it,
And go as a biscuit,
But a dog ate him up in the hall.

What happened to the criminal contortionist?

He turned himself in.

What did one parallel line say to the other?

'It's a shame we'll never meet.'

Why couldn't the bicycle stand up?
Because it was tyred.

What did the big chimney say to the little chimney?
You're too young to smoke.

Why couldn't the sailors play cards?
Because the captain was standing on the deck.

What do you give a sick bird?

Tweetment.

What has a bottom at the top?

A leg.

Pilot: Mayday! Mayday! Starboard engine on fire.

Ground control: State your height and position.

Pilot: I'm five foot nine and sitting in the cockpit.

What is worse than raining cats and dogs?

Hailing taxis.

What do you get if you cross a bridge with a car?

To the other side of the river.

Funny food

Why did the tomato blush?

Because he saw the salad dressing.

What kind of food does a racehorse eat?

Fast food.

What is square and green?

A lemon in disguise.

What's small and wobbly and sits in a pram?

A jelly baby.

Why did the egg go to the jungle?

Because it was an eggsplorer.

Why did the peanut go to the police?

Because he'd been assaulted.

What is small, round and giggles a lot?

A tickled onion.

What looks like half a loaf of bread?

The other half.

What do you call a mushroom who makes you laugh all day?

A fungi to be with.

How do you make a sausage roll?
Push it down the hill.

What's the fastest vegetable?
A runner bean.

How do you make an artichoke?
Strangle it.

What do Eskimos eat for breakfast?
Ice Krispies.

Why are cooks cruel?
Because they beat eggs and whip cream.

Have you seen the salad bowl?
No, but I've seen the lunch box.

A woman walked up to a man and tried to tell him that he had a leek sticking out of each ear. 'I'm sorry,' he said, 'I can't hear you. I've got a leek stuck in each ear.'

What do dieting cannibals eat?

Thin people.

What do you call two rows of vegetables?

A dual cabbage way.

What's white and fluffy and lives in the jungle?

A meringue-utan.

Why did the banana go to the doctor?

Because it wasn't peeling very well.

Big, grey elephant jokes

How does an elephant climb an oak tree?

He sits on an acorn and waits until spring.

What did the grape say when the elephant trod on it?

Nothing, it just let out a little wine.

What do you call an elephant with no teeth?

Gumbo.

What's the difference between a sleeping elephant and one that's awake?

With some elephants it's hard to tell.

Why do elephants live in the jungle?

Because they're too big to live in houses.

What do you get if you cross an elephant with a biscuit?

Crumbs.

What do you get if you cross an elephant with a bag of potatoes?

Mash.

What do elephants sing at Christmas?

Jungle bells, jungle bells.

What's big, heavy and grey and has sixteen wheels?

An elephant on roller skates.

What's the difference between a flea and an elephant?

An elephant can have fleas but a flea can't have elephants.

What do you get if you cross an elephant with a kangaroo?

Great big holes all over Australia.

What do you get if an elephant sits on your best friend?

A flat mate.

What did the peanut say to the elephant?

Nothing, peanuts can't talk.

What's the best way to catch an elephant?

Dress up like a cream bun and he'll follow you anywhere.

What is the same size and shape as an elephant but weighs nothing?

An elephant's shadow.

Why did the elephant tie a knot in his trunk?

To remind himself not to forget his hankie.

Why did the elephant go backwards into the telephone box?

He wanted to reverse the charges.

What is big, red and has a trunk?

An elephant with sunburn.

What's big, grey, heavy and wears glass slippers?

Cinderellaphant.

What is big, grey and protects you from the rain?

An umbrellaphant.

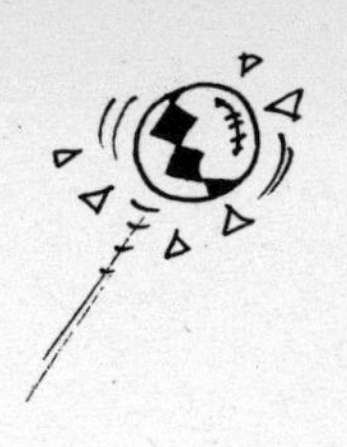

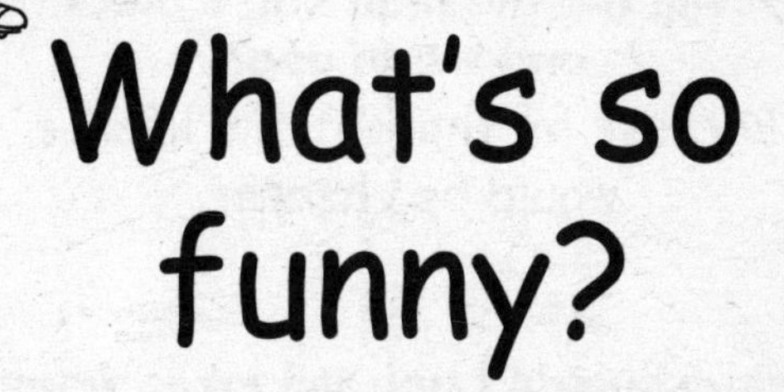

What's so funny?

What did Red Rum's jockey say at the end of the Grand National?

Whoaa!

What did the wall say to the plug?

Socket to me, baby!

What did the policeman say to his stomach?

You're under a vest.

How do you make a bandstand?

Hide all their chairs.

Why did the man buy a black and white dog?

Because he thought the licence would be cheaper.

Why shouldn't you tell jokes when you're ice-skating?

Because the ice might crack up.

What jumps from cake to cake and tastes of almonds?

Tarzipan.

Did you hear the one about the magic tractor?

It turned into a field.

Mum, Mum, can you see any change in me?
No, why?.
I've just swallowed 25p.

What nuts can be found in space?
Astronuts.

Why did the sailor grab a bar of soap when his ship was sinking?
He was hoping he'd be washed ashore.

What does the sea say to the sand?
Not much. It just waves.

What is wrapped in clingfilm and lives in a bell tower?
The lunch pack of Notre Dame.

Why do bees have sticky hair?
Because of their honey combs.

What do you call a robbery in Beijing?
A Chinese takeaway.

How do you make an apple puff?
Chase it round the garden.

Where does a general keep his armies?
Up his sleevies.

Why do wizards drink tea?
Because sorcerers need cuppas.

What is red and white?
Pink.

An Englishman, an Irishman and a Scotsman were all sentenced to death by firing squad.
The Englishman was brought out first and the firing squad took aim, when suddenly he yelled out, 'AVALANCHE!' In the confusion that followed he escaped.
Next the Scotsman thought he would try something similar and as the firing squad took aim he yelled, 'FLOOD!' And he too made his escape.
Finally it was the Irishman's turn. Confident of following in his friends' footsteps, as the firing squad took aim, he yelled, 'FIRE!'

What did one eye say to the other?
There's something between us that smells.

Why did the robber have a bath?
So he could make a clean getaway.

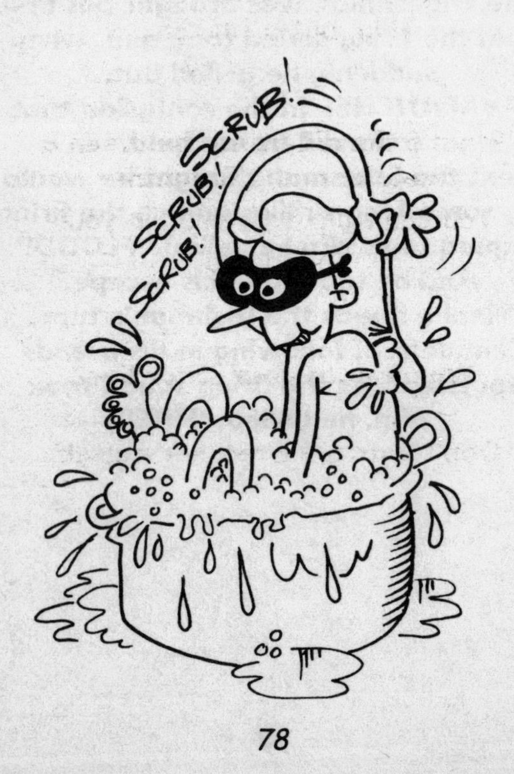

What did Cinderella say when she took her photos to be developed?

Some day my prints will come.

Can a shoe box?

No, but a tin can.

What's the difference between a soldier and a fireman?

You can't dip a fireman in your boiled egg.

Where does your sister live?

Alaska

Don't worry, I'll ask her myself.

Why is it difficult to keep a secret on a cold day?

Because you can't stop your teeth from chattering.

Why didn't anyone take the bus to school?

Because it wouldn't fit through the door.

What is brown and sticky?

A stick.

What is big, hairy and flies to New York faster than the speed of sound?

King Kongcorde.

What do you call high-rise flats for pigs?
Sty scrapers.

What sort of lights did Noah's Ark have?
Floodlights.

What do you call a boomerang that won't come back?

A stick.

Why did the cleaning lady stop work?

Because she found that grime doesn't pay.

Two pigeons were flying over a car dealer's yard one day and one said, 'Why don't we put a deposit on that Mercedes?'

Captain: We're sinking! Quick, send an SOS.

First mate: OK. How do you spell it?

Waiter, waiter . . .

Waiter, waiter, what's this fly doing on my ice cream?
Learning to ski I think, sir.

Waiter, waiter, bring me something to eat and make it snappy.

How about a crocodile sandwich, sir?

Waiter, waiter, how often do you change the tablecloths in this establishment?

I don't know, sir, I've only been here six months.

Waiter, waiter, this coffee tastes of mud!

That's perfectly natural, sir, after all it was only ground this morning.

Are you the same waiter who took my order?

Yes, sir.

My goodness, you've certainly aged well.

Waiter, waiter, what's wrong with this fish?

Long time, no sea, sir.

Waiter, waiter, how did this fly get in my soup?

It probably flew, madam.

Waiter, waiter, there's a fly in my soup!

That's OK, there's enough there for both of you.

Waiter, waiter, there's a fly in my ice cream!

Let him freeze to death, sir, it'll teach him a lesson.

Waiter: How did you find your steak sir?

Customer: Oh it wasn't difficult, it was just in between the potato and the salad.

Waiter, waiter, do you have frogs' legs?

Yes, sir.

Oh good. Can you hop over the counter and fix me a cheese sandwich?

Diner: What's that?

Waiter: It's a tomato surprise.

Diner: I can't see any tomatoes in it.

Waiter: I know, sir, that's the surprise.

Waiter, waiter, this soup's full of toadstools!

Yes, sir, I'm afraid there wasn't mushroom for many other ingredients.

Waiter, waiter, there's a button on my plate!

I'm sorry, sir, it must have fallen off the jacket potato.

Diner: Is this chicken or onion soup?

Waiter: Can't you tell by the flavour?

Diner: No.

Waiter: In that case, sir, does it make any difference?

Waiter, waiter, this egg is bad!
Don't blame me, sir, I only laid the table.

Waiter, waiter, why have you served me a squashed apple pie?
You said, 'Step on it, waiter, I'm in a hurry.'

Waiter, waiter, do you serve crabs in this restaurant?
We serve anyone, sir, please take a seat.

Waiter, waiter, do you have frogs' legs?
No, sir, I've always walked like this.

Waiter, waiter, there's a fly in my soup.
That's all right, sir, we won't charge you extra.

Waiter, waiter, how long will my sausages be?

About four inches, sir.

First customer: The service in this restaurant is terrible!

Second customer: I know, but the food is so bad I don't mind waiting for it.

Waiter, waiter, this soup tastes funny!

Then why aren't you laughing, sir?

Waiter, waiter, there's no chicken in this chicken pie!

Would you expect to find dog in a dog biscuit, sir?

Waiter, waiter, there's a small slug in my salad!

I do apologise, sir, would you like a bigger one?

Waiter, waiter, what's this fly doing in my soup?

It looks like backstroke to me, sir.

Waiter, waiter, I'm in a hurry – will my pancake be long?

No, sir, it will be round.

Waiter, waiter, there's a spider in my soup. Get me the manager!

That won't do any good, sir, he's afraid of them too.

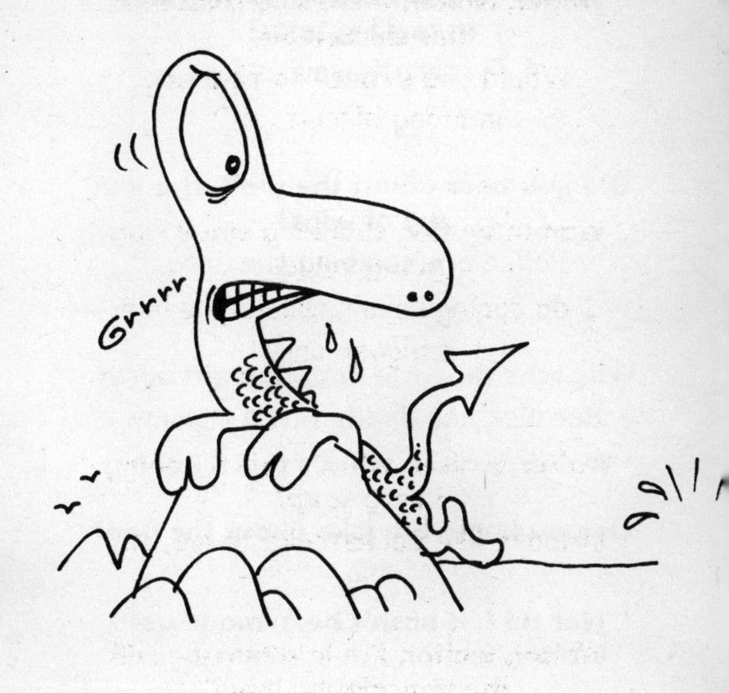

More laughs

What do you call a one-eyed dinosaur?

D'youthink'esaurus.

Which dinosaur always comes first in spelling tests?

A Tyrannathesaurus Rex.

Did you hear about the theft of a van full of wigs?

Police are combing the area.

Why was the little Egyptian girl upset.

Because her daddy was a mummy.

Do you know the joke about the bed?

No.

Nor do I, it hasn't been made yet!

Why did the two boa constrictors get married?

They had a crush on each other.

Why did the cowboy jump off the wagon?

Because he got stage fright.

Do you play the piano by ear?
No, I've always found it easier to use my hands.

Why did the man keep tripping over lobsters?
Because he was accident prawn.

Which vegetable is good at snooker?
A cue-cumber.

Why is the sky so high?
So birds don't bump their heads.

'I'd like to be included in your next edition,' said the man on the phone to the *Guinness Book of Records*. 'Why, what have you done?' came the reply. 'I've completed a jigsaw in just under a week and on the box it says three to five years.'

How do Eskimos dress?
As quickly as possible.

Why was the postman given the sack?
So he could carry letters in it.

What is big, green, bad-tempered and wears ripped clothes?
The Incredible Sulk.

Why did the tonsils get dressed up?
Because the doctor was taking them out.

How did the detective find Quasimodo?
He followed a hunch.

How do you get rid of a boomerang?
Throw it down a one-way street.

What do you call small rivers that run into the Nile?
Juveniles.

Teacher: What do you want to be when you grow up?

Boy: I want to follow in my father's footsteps and be a policeman.

Teacher: I didn't know your father was a policeman?

Boy: He's not, he's a burglar.

Why did the pilot crash into the house?

Because the landing light was left on.

What do you call a flying policeman?

A helicopper.

What is a crocodile's favourite game?

Snap.